Teach a

BEGINNING READER

with **Common Sense**

and a **Cookie Sheet**

A Guide for Parents

Melisa Buchanan

OAK PLANTATION PRESS

Published by Oak Plantation Press
P.O. Box 640
Rockwall, Texas 75087

Publisher's Cataloging in Publication
(Prepared by Quality Books Inc.)

Buchanan, Melisa, 1951
    Teach a beginning reader with common sense and a cookie sheet: a guide for parents/Melisa Buchanan.
p. cm.

ISBN 1-879129-00-0

1. Reading games. 2. Reading--Parent participation. 3. Reading--Phonetic method. I. Title

LB1050.4   649.58

                                        QB90-15
                                        MARC

Printed and bound in the United States of America.

ACKNOWLEDGMENT

I am most grateful to my husband, Barry, for his encouragement and support during this project. I also would like to acknowledge my three children, Matthew, Mindy and Beth for their patience and understanding, as well as their advice.

CONTENTS

INTRODUCTION

You, as parents, are your child's most important teachers. Young children learn best when they are able to have fun-filled experiences with games and activities. With no tedious workbooks, dittos or lengthy technical explanations, you can get your child on the right track to successful reading even before he starts school.

Your child's "classroom" can be as close as your kitchen, car or grocery store. With markers, file cards, chalk, magnetic letters and a cookie sheet, you can take advantage of time spent waiting for appointments and carpools to teach your child how to read!

Unfortunately, many parents (and some teachers, too) feel totally inadequate to teach early readers anything beyond their ABC's. Often parents believe that an attempt to help their children learn to read will only result in confusion and failure. "Leave it to the schools!" is the philosophy of some. But many four- and five-year olds are eager and ready to learn basic reading skills, and there are parents who want to help them. This book is designed to show you just how you can affect your child's reading success through playtime experiences. Given the appropriate knowledge and ideas, you can create meaningful educational experiences that will last a lifetime.

As a mother of three, a former teacher and an academic therapist, I find myself frustrated by educational materials available for beginning readers. Most materials offer a variety of skills presented in a scattered, illogical order which provide the child little information about letter and sound relationships. No matter how colorful or enticing the illustrations, the child will not likely benefit from such hit-or-miss materials.

Most importantly, a child will be at a severe disadvantage if he never learns how letters work together to make words. He needs to feel secure with a system on which he can rely when he encounters unfamiliar words. One thing I have noticed year after year is that many children simply do not have a tool to decipher unknown words. They do not know what to do when faced with an unfamiliar word, so they guess! A child can not comprehend words that he can not begin to identify.

The philosophy of this book is simple: Children need to understand the process of how individual letters and sounds make words. Even though the English language can seem complex and inconsistent, my belief is that a child will benefit greatly when reading is first taught in a controlled environment that allows him to be successful in its consistencies. Then, gradually, the inconsistencies of the language can be introduced. This is a step-by-step approach that combines writing and spelling skills as well so that the child can understand their integral relationship. It is a technique that lessens the chance of a child falling into the gaps of a well-intentioned educational system.

Though the ideas of this book have a phonetic foundation, I almost hesitate to use that word: PHONICS! Many suffer from an enormous misconception about phonics. To those people, phonics equates only to laborious dissections of words and stacks of workbook pages, quite a distasteful thought! That is NOT the focus nor intent of this book.

Therefore, I will not dwell on the term PHONICS but instead on a logical progression of phonetic skill-builders that can make even the non-believers forget that they are applying phonics. These phonetic skills will become automatic, a habit. With no overly-technical lists of rules and exceptions, this is truly PHONICS MADE FUN AND EASY!

To those who still would cry, "Boring! Monotonous!", I say, "Hogwash!" Learning experiences, even involving phonics, can certainly be FUN, particularly when the atmosphere is relaxed, informal and supportive. Learning time can be playtime when the activities are well-planned yet teach in a spirit of spontaneity. As a result, your child will have the key to unlock words for his lifetime.

Very often a young school-aged reader is restricted to the stories in a basal reading series because he is being taught predominantly by sight memorization. When the child wants to read from even a simple library book, he may be disappointed because it contains many words he has not yet been taught. However, with the mastery of these phonetic skills, he will be able to enter the world of library books, magazines and limitless other materials much earlier than many of his peers. The more resources he is able to read, the greater the opportunities for expanding his vocabulary and thinking skills. What a special gift to give your child!

Parent's Promises:

The following list of parental promises is absolutely invaluable to your child's reading growth. Your involvement in these areas cannot be over-emphasized. Make a promise to your child to:

1. Read to him daily! If you are not already doing so, begin to set aside a special time each day to share a book with your child. As a reading model,

you will demonstrate examples of fluency (smoothness) and inflection (changes in voice pitch), as well as vocabulary enrichment and pure enjoyment!

2. Let him see you read everyday! Particularly in this day of electronic technology, it is imperative that you show how you value written words. Read newspapers, magazines and books, and make certain that your child sees you!

3. Surround him with books and other written materials and supplies for writing, such as a chalkboard, chalk, markers, highlighters, a marker board, and lots of paper. These are vital to the reading and writing environment.

Some educators stress that the words a child first learns to read must be meaningful to his life experiences. I stress that the words will become most meaningful when the child is able to read independently from any of the exciting materials found in his environment: books, signs, menus, game directions, textbooks, newspapers, etc. If we thoughtfully and carefully teach a child these word-building skills, he will have a much greater chance to succeed.

Chapter 1

WHERE DO I BEGIN?

Most of us take for granted the act of learning to read. We are not aware of the process that led us to reading independently. "Where do I begin?" is a common question from those who want to teach a child to read.

In order to provide a beginning reader with a strong sense of security and consistency, each letter of the alphabet will be introduced with only one specific sound. In order to read, the child needs to recognize each letter and associate its sound.

Example:
> For the letter **f** you will say,
> "This is the letter **f**.
> It says **f-f-f** as in fan."

As you make this introduction, write the letter **f** so that your child can see how the letter is made. (See pages 70-71 for correct letter formation.) Let him make the letter using colored chalk, marker or any enticing writing tool. Then, have him repeat the

1

letter name and sound and write the letter on a chalkboard, marker board, file card, etc. When you pronounce the individual sounds, be very certain NOT to tag extra sounds onto the first. For example, do not turn the **f-f-f** sound into **fuh-uh** or **m-m-m** into **muh-uh**. It is an easy mistake to make, but try to keep each sound uncluttered by other sounds.

Also, if the child has difficulty in forming the written letters, help him by making a dot-to dot pattern to follow until he is able to do it on his own.

In this chapter and those that follow, you will find many games and activities which will give practice and reinforcement for the first seven letters to be introduced. You may wonder why the first letters are f, m, n, a, s, h, and v instead of the first seven letters of the alphabet: a, b, c, d, e, f, and g. Simply stated, sounds that can be made continually are the easiest to blend together, so some of those sounds will be taught first. This will facilitate the child's ability to sound-blend words. Very quickly the child will be able to make and blend words such as: fan, man, Nan, van, am, Sam and ham. These words are examples of the Consonant-Vowel-Consonant or **CVC** words that will be used throughout the first several chapters. At this point it is important to note that the terms "vowel" and "consonant" should be explained very simply. Vowels are basically the letters a, e, i, o, and u. The consonants are the remaining letters of the alphabet. Also, there is nothing sacred about the order of the letter introduction but this approach assures consistency, no hit-or-miss technique.

CHAPTER 1 LETTERS AND SOUNDS

1.	**f**	**f-f-f**	as in fan
2.	**m**	**m-m-m**	as in man
3.	**n**	**n-n-n**	as in nut
4.	**a**	**a-a-a**	as in apple
5.	**s**	**s-s-s**	as in Sam
6.	**h**	**h-h-h**	as in hat
7.	**v**	**v-v-v**	as in van

Notice that a KEY WORD has been designated for each letter and sound so that the child can return to it if he is unable to recreate the sound from memory.

CHAPTER 1 WORD SUGGESTIONS

fan

man

Nan

van

am

Sam

ham

After the letter names and sounds have been introduced, use the following activities until the child has mastered them. You might begin working with just the first two letters and add one at a time until all seven letters have been mastered. Some children may feel pressured if more than one letter is introduced in a week while others may be able to handle several letters/sounds in one session. MOVE ONLY AS FAST AS THE CHILD'S ABILITY ALLOWS. If he shows stress and great uncertainty, CHANGE ACTIVITIES. Be sure to keep the atmosphere pleasant and fun! Expectations that are too high will quickly lead to frustration and failure. The length of time required to master all of these skills will vary with each individual. More important than the length of time needed is that he learn these skills as a foundation to any other reading program.

GAMES AND ACTIVITIES TO USE FOR CHAPTER 1

These are designed to follow the introduction
of the first seven letters.

Please understand that these activities may be repeated daily or as often as needed for reinforcement and mastery. The variations are endless, so be creative! Modify them to meet the individual needs of your child.

Also, NEVER make fun of or criticize the efforts of your child. With your support and patience he will flourish, but he will be crippled by criticism and pressure. Relax and have fun together!

1. COOKIE SHEET FUN: Place colorful magnetic letters on a cookie sheet. Plastic magnetic letters can be purchased at most toy or discount stores. Try to find those letters that include both lower and upper cases and that are made as those

shown on pages 70-71. However, use only the lower case letters for these first activities. The upper case letters will be introduced and reinforced in later chapters. For this game, use the first two letters, **f** and **m**. Say to your child,

"Show me the letter **m**."

As he points to the letter, encourage him to also say the letter name and to make the sound of the letter,

"**M** says **m-m-m** as in man."

If he is hesitant, go back to the introductory phrase and key word and repeat.

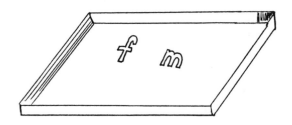

2. GUESS WHICH HAND: Try hiding one of the letters in your hand. Let the child guess which letter it might be, then open your hand to let him check. Children love to guess, and this is another way of reinforcing these two letters/sounds. When your child shows that he is comfortable with these first two sounds, move on the next activities.

3. MORE COOKIE SHEET FUN: Now vary the
    cookie sheet activity somewhat as you gradually
    add the remaining letters of CHAPTER 1. Using
    several letters now, have the child find the letter
    that makes the sound you demonstrate. Say,

    "Pick up the letter that makes this sound: **h-h-h**."
    "Great! Now find the one that says, **a-a-a**."

    "I bet you can't find the one that says, **v-v-v**.
    Wow, you did it!" (Kids love to beat you!)

    Continue to rearrange the letters until all seven
    CHAPTER 1 letters have been used. If there are
    letters/sounds that are causing particular problems,
    isolate those letters and repeat the activities with just
    those letters until the child is comfortable with them.
    Remember, these activities can be used several times
    daily in short doses.

    Here are more activities that will help with mastery of
    CHAPTER 1 letters and sounds.

4. LETTER TAKE-AWAY: Place several of the
    magnetic letters (or use file cards and print the
    letters) in front of your child. Have him tell you
    the name of each letter and its sound. Then, let
    him cover his eyes while you remove one of the
    letters. Have him open his eyes and tell you the
    SOUND of the letter that is missing. As he is
    able, add more letters until you are using all

seven CHAPTER 1 letters. It is important not to increase the number of letters too quickly! We want him to feel successful, not frustrated. It is also fun to reverse the activity and let the CHILD remove a letter and have YOU figure out which one is missing. Almost always, children like to play the role of the ''teacher.''

5. WHICH IS WHICH?: On a chalkboard or file card, write a row of the CHAPTER 1 letters. Use each letter several times in a random order. Example:

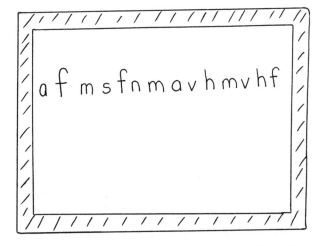

Have the child find and circle all the **f**'s. Then write another row of letters and have him look for one of the other CHAPTER 1 letters. This activity is particularly helpful if a child is having some difficulty in visually distinguishing between letter symbols. Also, try the same activity but ask the child to circle all the letters that make the **v-v-v** sound (or **s-s-s** sound, **n-n-n** sound, etc.).

6. CAN YOU FEEL IT?: Place several of the magnetic letters in a bag or box. Let the child put his hand in, pick one letter and try to guess which letter it is before he takes the letter out of the bag. Have him also tell you the sound it makes.

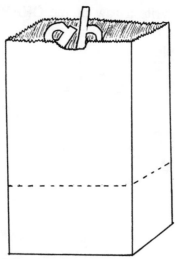

7. COVER UP: Using a file card and marker, write the seven CHAPTER 1 letters in squares. As you make the sound of each letter, let the child cover the printed letter with a coin, bean or game chip. Then, when all seven are covered, have him uncover them one at a time and tell you the name and the sound. This is a preliminary step to BINGO, which will be used in CHAPTER 2.

8. WRITE IT IN SAND: Fill a cake pan with sand, salt, cornmeal or such. Let the child practice writing the letter that you pronounce. Remember that correct letter formation is illustrated on pages 70-71. Have him say the name and sound of each letter as he writes it. Watch carefully as the child makes each letter. It is much easier to create a good habit than it is to try to correct a bad habit later.

9.   SIDEWALK WRITING: Use chalk on your sidewalk or driveway as an entertaining way to sharpen those writing skills. Have your child make the letters as you give him the sounds. It is important for the child to experience the actual writing of letters as he pronounces them. This is a fun way to perfect the correct writing strokes: where to begin each letter, in which direction it goes, how tall it should be in relation to other letters.

10.   WHAT DO YOU HEAR?: To sharpen auditory skills, have the child listen carefully as you say,

"What sound do you hear at the BEGINNING of **fan**?"

"What sound do you hear at the BEGINNING of **hat**?"

"What sound do you hear at the END of **Pam**?"

"What sound do you hear at the END of **van**?"

"What sound do you hear in the MIDDLE of **Sam**?"

Continue with other words in the same manner. This activity easily lends itself to riding in the car or waiting in line at the bank.

11. CLAP AND SNAP: This activity is a variation of #10. Have the child clap, snap fingers, stomp feet, etc. when he hears the "designated letter sound." Example:

"Johnny, I want you to clap your hands if you hear me use this sound: **h-h-h**."

Then proceed to make the various sounds of the CHAPTER 1 letters. Pronounce each sound slowly and clearly before moving to the next sound.

f-f-f, m-m-m, v-v-v, s-s-s, n-n-n, a-a-a

If the child is successful, you may want to change his response so that one time he claps, the next time he stomps, and the next time he whistles.

Make the activity a bit more difficult by using words instead of individual letters. Example:

"Johnny, this time I want you to snap your fingers anytime you hear me use the **v-v-v** sound in a word."

This time, use a list of words instead of letters. Have him respond to the **v-v-v** sound as he hears it in the words.

mat, pan, van, sad, mad, met, vet, mud, net, vat

Again, continue with similar lists.

12. MAKE-A-WORD: Now comes the really exciting part of teaching a beginning reader! When your child has mastered the CHAPTER 1 letters and sounds, you are ready to show him just how easy it is to MAKE-A-WORD! This activity is one of the most valuable experiences your child will have as a reader because it demonstrates HOW individual letters work together to make words!

Display all seven CHAPTER 1 letters on the cookie sheet. Ask the child to pick out the letter that would make the **f-f-f** sound. When he gives you the letter **f**, place it away from the remaining letters. (If he has difficulty, just go back to the KEY WORDS and have him repeat those beginning sounds.) Then ask him to pick out the letter that makes the **a-a-a** sound. Next, have him pick out the letter that makes the **n-n-n** sound. Using only the letters **f**, **a**, and **n**, display them in that order. Then have the child make the sound of each one as you point to it moving from left to right.

f   a   n

f-f-f a-a-a n-n-n

Demonstrate how to blend the sounds more quickly so that together they make **fan**. It may be helpful to push the letters together as he sounds them out in order to understand the blending process. Use the following words in the same manner to practice blending:

fan, man, Nan, van, am, Sam, and ham

Notice that two proper names, Nan and Sam, are included. It is not important to emphasize capital letters at this time. Simply explain that names of people will begin with capital letters and that this is what these particular letters look like. In later chapters, capital letters are addressed with activities.

13. CREATE-YOUR-OWN-GAME-BOARDS: Here is an easy-to-make game that you can create with unlined 5x7 file cards or art board and some colorful labeling stickers. Write the CHAPTER 1 words on labeling stickers and arrange them on the card as a game board. Repeat the words as many times as necessary in order to complete your game board.

Be as creative or as simple as you like. Then, you will need either a spinner or dice and game markers. (Borrow these from another game or use household objects such as a penny and a dime.) Playing with your child, move your markers according to the number that each of you rolls, then sound-blend the word written on the space. Continue to the finish line.

Make these games appropriate to the reading level of the child. Continue to make new games as additional letters and sounds are introduced.

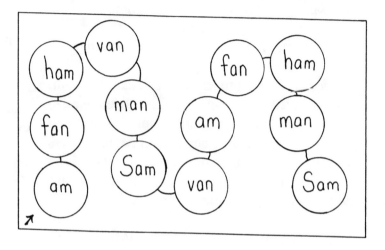

Chapter 2

NOW WHAT?

The logical progression of letter/sound introduction continues in CHAPTER 2. Introduce each of the next six letters with its sound as in Chapter 1. It is still important to demonstrate how to write the letter as the sound is being made. Remember to say to the child:

> "This is the letter o. It makes the sound o-o-o like in octopus."

CHAPTER 2 LETTERS AND SOUNDS

1.	o	o-o-o	as in octopus
2.	l	l-l-l	as in lip
3.	w	w-w-w	as in wet
4.	t	t	as in top
5.	p	p	as in pan
6.	b	b	as in bat

Notice that t, p, and b do NOT have continuous sounds. Simply, they are called stop sounds. Now, vary the introduction routine by using different textured materials for the letters. Those made of felt or sandpaper can provide opportunities for the child to feel the letter shapes. This can be a meaningful tactile experience. Also remember to have the child write the letter as he is saying the name and sound. Continue to use a variety of writing materials.

As more letters are introduced, you may notice that some combinations of letters such as **ow** in **low** do not keep with the **o** sound as in **octopus**. Do not be overly concerned. The **ow** pattern will be introduced later as a LETTER PARTNER. For now, continue with the CVC words that remain true to the sounds that you have introduced.

CHAPTER 2 CVC WORD SUGGESTIONS

These are suggested words to get you started. There are, of course, others that you can make.

lab	tam	pan	lap	bat	sob	hop	hot
tab	pal	tan	map	fat	mob	mop	lot
		van	nap	hat	pop	not	
			tap	mat	top	pot	

Be sure to continue MAKE-A-WORD activities as described in Chapter 1. In addition, use the following games and activities for sound-blending practice and understanding.

GAMES AND ACTIVITIES TO USE FOR CHAPTERS 1 AND 2

These are designed to use with letters:
f,m,n,a,s,h,v,l,o,w,t,p,b

1. BINGO: Use 5x7 index cards to make your own Bingo game. Write CVC words from the above letters in each of the nine squares on the Bingo card. (Later, use all of the letters as they are introduced.) Make several different game cards so that others in the family can play. Write each of the CVC word possibilities on a slip of paper, then place the papers in a container. Take turns being the "caller" who draws a slip of paper and reads the word. Cover the words with game chips, coins or beans. A horizontal, vertical or diagonal row makes a winner!

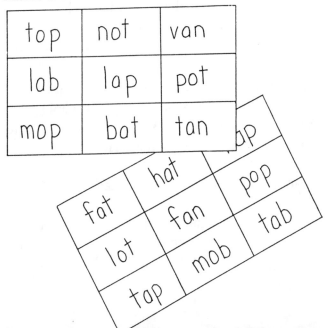

2. FIND THAT WORD: Make your own word-hunt games by marking rows of squares on cards or papers. Write CVC words from Chapters 1 and 2 in the squares and fill in the extra squares with more letters. Have the child hunt for any CVC words that he can find and have him circle each one with colorful markers. Then have him sound-blend each word and read it to you.

l	a	p	b	s
v	h	o	t	p
n	s	b	a	t

3. HERE'S A CLUE!: To extend vocabulary and to reinforce those CVC words, play this simple game. Write the following six CVC words on a file card: man, pan, tan, tam, van, mat. Then say,

    "I'm thinking of a word that means . . .

a light brown color."	(tan)
a flat cap or hat."	(tam)
something that I cook in."	(pan)

something I might drive.''   (van)
what a boy grows up into.'' (man)
something I might nap on.'' (mat)

Let the child be a detective as he uses those clues to match each word with its description.

4. CAN I TRICK YOU?: This activity sharpens visual discrimination as well as listening skills. Present this game in the spirit of ''I'm going to trick you!''. Using the letters already introduced, write three similar CVC words on a chalkboard, marker board or file card. Example:

lab
lap
lot

Pronounce one of the words and let the child circle it with chalk or marker. If he has difficulty with this game, you will need to repeat some of the earlier cookie sheet activities until he is more sure of himself. Then, continue to make up your own ''tricks'' for extra practice.

top	pot
pop	top
tap	pat
hot	mop
hop	man
pot	map

5. FLASHCARD FLIP: This game paces the child against himself and builds automatic word recognition. Write each of the Chapter 1 and 2 words on a 3x5 file card. Use a stop watch to time your child as he pronounces all of the cards in the stack. Record the time. Repeat this activity daily if possible and see the time get faster and faster. Children love to start and stop the watch. Keep the cards handy for those times when you have to wait for an appointment or carpool. Additional cards can easily be made for future chapters.

6. IT'S MAGIC: With an imaginative wand (a dowel rod, paper towel tube or baton), your child can perform wonderful magic with the words from Chapters 1 and 2. He may even want to cover his trick with a scarf or a towel. Using a chalkboard or marker board, have him write a word such as **web**. Then with an "**abracadabra**," have him turn **web** into **wet** by changing the **b** to **t**. He will proudly display his "magic" as he reads the new word.

Just think of all the possibilities by changing the beginning, middle or ending sound each time.

"Turn **sit** into **sat**."
"Turn **sat** into **fat**."
"Turn **fat** into **fan**."
"Turn **fan** into **pan**."
"Turn **pan** into **pin**."   (etc.)

7. SCRAMBLE: On blue file cards, write the vowels **a** and **o**. Then write the remaining letters from Chapters 1 and 2 on white file cards. Turn all of the cards face down and have the child scramble the cards. Next, let him choose two white cards and one blue card to turn over. Arrange them so that the blue vowel card is in the middle. Let the child sound-blend the word. Be sure to pronounce the sounds as the child has learned even if they make a nonsense word. If by chance the cards chosen display **o** and **w**, be sure to place **w** first in order to keep the sounds true to a CVC pattern as previously discussed.

8. RHYME TIME: It is important that the child learn to identify rhyming words. To develop his auditory discrimination skills, play some fun listening games. Initially, you may need to exaggerate the sounds to help the child distinguish between those that rhyme and those that do not. It may also be helpful for the child to close his eyes so that he can concentrate fully on these sounds. Ready? Pronounce these two words from Chapters 1 and 2.

man   top

Now, ask the child, "Do those words sound alike in any way?" If he has difficulty in distinguishing the differences, repeat the words. Let the child say the words with you until he hears the difference.

Now pronounce these two words:

man   van

Again ask the child, "Do these words sound alike?" Explain that these two words rhyme because they have the same sounds at the end: **an**. Continue with other word pairs and let the child tell you if the two words rhyme or not. Examples:

lot and sob	fan and tan
hat and lot	Nan and man
mop and top	mob and mat
top and tap	tam and Pam

For more auditory practice, pronounce any of the Chapter 1 or 2 words. Let the child make as many rhyming matches as he can. It is fine if he comes up with rhyming words that are nonsense words or that are not in Chapters 1 or 2. The primary goal is to recognize the rhyming sounds in all words.

Chapter 3

NOW I'VE GOT IT!

The next six letters should be introduced as soon as the Chapters 1 and 2 letters and sounds have been mastered. Remember to continue the same introductory process as in the earlier chapters. Say to the child:

"This is the letter **i**. It says **i-i-i** as in Indian."

CHAPTER 3 LETTERS AND SOUNDS

1. **i**	**i-i-i**	as in Indian
2. **d**	**d**	as in dot
3. **c**	**c**	as in cap
4. **g**	**g**	as in gum
5. **u**	**u-u-u**	as in umbrella
6. **j**	**j**	as in jet
7. **z**	**z-z-z**	as in zip

Later, you can point out that both **c** and **g** have different sounds in some words like **city** and **giraffe**.

Substitute the Chapter 3 letters and sounds for those in the Chapters 1 and 2 activities such as COOKIE SHEET

FUN. Continue until the child has a recognition and understanding of the Chapter 3 letters and sounds. Then proceed with these additional activities using the letters of all three chapters. You will be amazed at the number of word possibilities! With practice and reinforcement, the child will begin to "let go" of the sound-blending process and will read more automatically and fluently.

CHAPTER 3 CVC WORD SUGGESTIONS

and	bad	bag	dam	not	bid	dip	gum	sun
cab	dad	lag	jam	lot	did	hip	hum	gun
cop	had	nag	can	pot	hid	lip	jug	up
hop	lad	sag	cap	got	lid	nip	bug	bus
mop	mad	tag	gap	dot	big	sip	dug	hug
top	pad	wag	mob	jot	dig	tip	tug	lug
pop	sad	fog	sob	bib	pig	pin	bun	tub
sop	mom	hog	job	fib	wig	tin	fun	sub
zag	zap	zig	zip					

Remember, there are other words you can make using these letters. These are just suggestions.

GAMES AND ACTIVITIES TO USE FOR CHAPTERS 1, 2, AND 3

These are designed to use with letters:
f,m,n,a,s,h,v,l,o,w,t,p,b,i,d,c,g,u,j,z

1. TREASURE HUNT: This is a fun way to use those sound-blending skills. Write any of the CVC words from Chapters 1, 2, and 3 on slips of paper. Hide

them in the room or even outside. Let your child search for his "treasures" and then read them to you. You might even give a small treat as an additional motivation. Also, gear this game to holidays or seasons. For example, cut the slips of paper into holiday shapes such as Easter eggs, pumpkins or snowflakes.

As the child becomes more skillful, expand this activity. Write phrases or simple sentences to encourage extended reading.

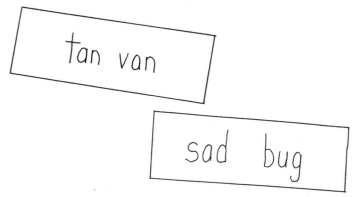

2. BLOCK IT: Use three cubical gift wrap boxes to
    create a game that reinforces word-building skills.
    On each side of two of the cubes, write a
    consonant letter that has been introduced. On each
    side of the third cube, write a vowel introduced
    previously: a,o,i and u. Obviously you will have to
    repeat some letters. Write the vowels in a different
    color so that they are distinguished from the
    consonants.

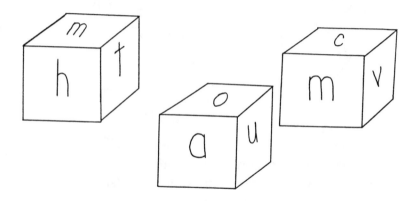

Making certain that the vowel cube is in the
middle, let the child "roll" the cubes. Then have
him sound-blend the resulting words. Some of the
words may be "nonsense" words. For example, if
he rolls the word **hib**, let him pronounce it as he
would any other word. Nonsense words are great
for the child to demonstrate just how well he
understands the relationship between letters and
sounds, so it is important that he go ahead and
sound-blend them. Just be sure to point out that
they are "silly-willy" words.

3. CONFIGURE-IT: A way to encourage visual discrimination is to play a game that helps the child understand the size relationships and formations of letters. First explain to him how some letters are only one-story tall: n,s and a.

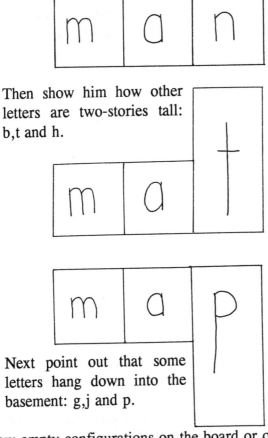

Then show him how other letters are two-stories tall: b,t and h.

Next point out that some letters hang down into the basement: g,j and p.

Draw empty configurations on the board or on a card and let the child think of his own words that would fit the configuration. Write all of the Chapters 1-3 letters at the top so that he can refer to them if he so needs.

4. COOKIE WALK: Now THIS is an activity sure to please a youngster. Write any of the CVC words from Chapters 1-3 on file cards. Tape the file cards to the floor or sidewalk. As you do with Musical Chairs, have the child walk around the path while music is playing. When the music stops, have him step on the nearest card and sound-blend its word. Recognize his winning efforts with a cookie and play again.

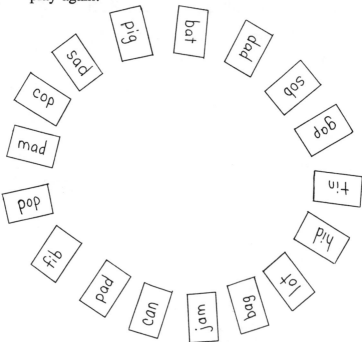

5. DINOSAUR DANCE: This is a slight variation of the COOKIE WALK. Write the words or phrases on cut-outs of dinosaur feet. Use your imagination! Children love to add their own dinosaur movements.

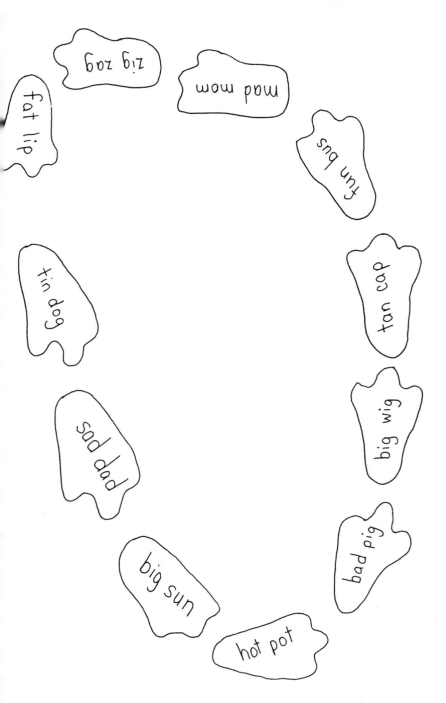

6. TWIST AND TURN: Let the child use pipecleaners to form letters. You can give him a specific sound and have him form the corresponding letter. Then, let him put letters side-by-side to make words.

fib

mad

hid

top

7. PLAY WITH CLAY: As with the above activity, let the child make letters from shaping clay or playdough. He can make words and even phrases from the letters of Chapters 1-3.

8. RHYME TIME TWO: For a more difficult version of a rhyming activity, pronounce three words from Chapters 1-3, two that rhyme and one that does not. Example:

dig   job   wig

Let the child tell you which one does not rhyme. You can also expand this activity by adding a fourth word.

Chapter 4

WE'RE ALMOST THERE!

These last six letters complete the alphabet introduction. Continue to use the familiar statement to introduce each of the letters and sounds. Say to the child:

"This is the letter **e**. It makes the sound of **e-e-e** like in elephant."

CHAPTER 4 LETTERS AND SOUNDS

1. e	e-e-e	as in elephant
2. k	k	as in kit
3. r	r-r-r	as in red
4. y	y-y-y	as in yellow
5. x	x	as in box (note the sound is at the END of this sample word)
6. qu	qu	as in queen (note that q will always be shown with u)

CHAPTER 4 CVC WORD SUGGESTIONS

Now you can use any letter needed to make true CVC words! Here are some more suggestions to add to the growing list of CVC words. Remember, this is only a partial list.

bed	peg	rag	run	nix
beg	pet	ram	rut	six
bet	pen	ran	yam	box
den	pep	rap	yap	fox
fed	red	rat	yum	pox
get	set	rib	sax	tux
hen	ten	rid	tax	quip
jet	vet	rig	wax	quit
led	web	rim	hex	quiz
let	wed	rip	vex	yip
men	yes	rob	fix	Jed
net	yet	rug	mix	Max
Ken	kid	kit	Kix	Kip

    *You man also take the opportunity to point out words such as fell, bell, will, and hill which double the last consonant. This does not change the sound or pronunciation of such words.

WEIRD WORDS!

    In order to write sentences that incorporate the CVC words, it will be helpful to now introduce some of the irregular words from our English language. An effective way to deal with these words is to introduce only a few at a time and to distinguish them in a fun and silly way. Let's call them WEIRD WORDS and designate them as such by drawing a funny cloud around each one. For this chapter, we will use only the following 5 WEIRD WORDS. More of these words will be introduced in the following chapters.

1. was   4. to

2. the   5. said

3. a

Begin by explaining to the child that you are going to show him some really funny words called WEIRD WORDS. Simply explain that these words do not stay true to the sounds of their letters and that they must be memorized. Until the child has mastered these WEIRD WORDS, it is important to draw the cloud around these words to differentiate them from the true CVC words. This will help avoid confusion.

Example:

A big red fox was in the pit.

GAMES AND ACTIVITIES TO USE FOR CHAPTERS 1,2,3 AND 4

These activities are designed to use with CVC words made from any of the letters of the alphabet: a,b,c,d,e,f,g,h,i,j,k,l,m,n,o,p,q,r,s,t,u,v,w,x,y,z

1. ALPHABET MANIA: Now that the child is familiar with all the letters of the alphabet, it is time to make certain that he knows them in the ABC order. Use all of the magnetic letters and mix them up. Then let the child arrange them in the ABC order on the cookie sheet.

   In a spirit of "tricking", see if your child can answer the following questions.

   "What letter comes just after l?"

   "What letter comes just after y?"

   "What letter comes just before d?"

   "What letter comes just before p?"

   "Would I find the letter e toward the beginning or the end of the alphabet?"

   Continue with similar questions. If the child needs to see the ABC letters sequenced on the cookie sheet, permit him to do that in the early stages of this game, but gradually remove that crutch so that he is completing the task without a visual aid.

2. NONSENSE NOODLE: Let your child sound out and write these nonsense words. Remember to vary the writing supplies: crayons, markers, colored pens, chalk, etc.

muz   gav   quib
nid   tig   rax
fop   vub   bof

Then let the child make up his own nonsense words. This can get quite silly!

3. MATCH 'EM UP!: Since most of the capital letters resemble their lower case counterparts, the child probably already recognizes many of the capital letters. However, take this opportunity to introduce any of those that may yet be unfamiliar by using both the capital and lower case letters on the cookie sheet. Let the child match each lower case letter to its capital. It is also important that he practice writing these letters as well. Follow the correct letter formation guide on pages 70-71. Then encourage him to use those new writing skills in as many situations as possible.

4. ALPHABET DRAW: Next, make two sets of playing cards from unruled file cards. On each of the first set, write a lower case letter of the alphabet. On each of the second set, write a corresponding capital letter. Now shuffle all 52 cards in one stack. Deal 8 cards to each player, and place the remaining cards in a stack, face down. Then, take turns drawing one card at a time from the stack. If you have a capital letter that matches its lower case letter, you have a pair. Turn each pair face up, and continue to play until all of the cards have been used. The player with the

greater number of pairs is the winner. It may also be helpful to have the child tell the name of the letter and the sound it makes.

5. FOLD-A-FAN: Fold strips of paper at least 18" long into about 15 accordion folds. Have the child write a CVC word on each fold. Return to the folded position, then let him unfold each word and read it as quickly as he can. It's a simple but fun way to practice those newly-learned skills!

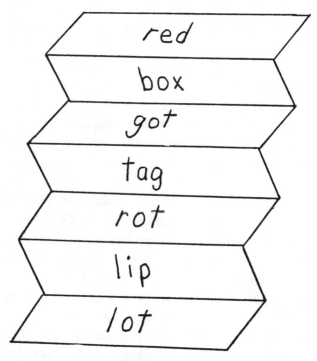

6. MARK THE NEWS: Give the child a newspaper and a marker. Let him find as many CVC words as possible.

7. SENTENCE STRIPS: To encourage extended and more fluid reading, use sentence strips. Make your own strips, approximately 3''x 18'', from poster board, manila paper or construction paper. Write a complete sentence on each strip using the words from Chapters 1-4. Glide your fingers from left to right under the words to help train his eyes in the reading movement. Use the following examples for the strips and then be sure to create your own as well.

The pet was in the pen.

Ten men got in wet mud.

The red fox sat on a big rug.

8. STORY CARDS: Once your child has mastered sentence strips, you can write your own story cards for him or even let him help. Using the numerous CVC words available and the 5 Weird Words, see how many fun and silly stories you can write. It is a good idea to print these on 5x7 file cards and to let the child illustrate them.

Example 1:

Pam and Dad had the tan van in a big dip. Dad was mad at the van. It had no gas.

Pam and Dad had to run to get gas. Pam had a gas can. Dad had a map.

Pam and Dad got gas on the hill. Yes, the van did run. But, the job was not fun!

Example 2:

Sam the cat was fat. Sam had a lot of ham and pop! Sam did not run. Sam sat on a mat in the hot sun.

Sam did not nap. Sam was mad at the sun. Sam got a big, BIG hat! Sam was not hot. Sam had a nap.

Example 3:

Ted was a fat pig. Ted had a red wig. Ted sat on a big log in a pit.

Ted had a bib on, but it was a mess! Ted got jam and ham on him.

Example 4:

Jim the rat sat in mud. It was wet, and it was not fun.

Jim got in a box on a rug. Jim was not wet. Jim was not sad. Jim had a nap.

Example 5:

Kit the cat got in a hut. Kit got a nut and a bat.

Kit hit the nut. Bam! Bam! Kit had the nut. Yum! Yum!

Example 6:

Jed and a dog sat in the den. Jed let the pet sit on top of a big bag. "Yap! Yap!" said Dan the dog.

Jed got mad at Dan. "Bad dog!" said Jed. Jed got rid of the dog.

Dan the dog sat on a tan rug. "Yap! Yap!" said Dan. "Bad, bad dog!" said Jed.

Dan got in Jed's lap. He had a nap, and Jed was not mad.

Chapter 5

LETTER PARTNERS
WORK TOGETHER!

When the child has mastered the letters and sounds of the first four chapters, he should be able to read any true CVC word with little effort. Once he can, he is ready to tackle the next step: LETTER PARTNERS! Instead of technical definitions of diagraphs, dipthongs, blends or irregular vowel sounds, we will simplify the procedure by introducing certain letters as "partners that work together."

Explain that when certain letters join together, they make a partner sound. Some of these partners will be two vowels that work together, such as **ai** in **rain** or **oi** in **oil**. Other partners will be two consonants, such as **bl** in **black**. Still others will be formed by several letters such as **igh** in **night**. Sometimes certain letter combinations will create a slight distortion of the sounds, but do not to draw special attention to those partners as usually the child will be unaffected by such minor changes. (Examples of those combinations are **ang**, **ing**, and **ung**.)

The most important thing is that the child learn to recognize these LETTER PARTNERS and that he be able to relate a sound to a specific set of letters. By recalling these partners, the child will have a useful tool to use when faced with unfamiliar or complicated words. This approach is not meant to minimize the value of a technical understanding of such patterns, but to overburden a child with complicated explanations is unnecessary when a very simple approach serves the purpose well.

Ultimately, we want your child to know how to decode unfamiliar words so that he can comprehend them. The child will have an advantage even when the sounds vary slightly from the true sounds as he has learned them.

*There is one point that needs to be addressed before continuing with LETTER PARTNERS. Some short words will end with a vowel that says its name. (Remember that sometimes **y** will act as a vowel.) For example:

be	go	by
me	no	fly
he	so	cry
she	ho-ho	my

At this stage, just make the child aware of this particular word type as a situation arises. Now on to LETTER PARTNERS!

GROUP 1 PARTNERS: The first set of partners to be introduced will be those in which an **r** follows a vowel.

Example: For the partners **ar** you will say,
"These are the letter partners **ar**.
Together, they will say **ar** as in car.

ar	as in car
or	as in corn
er	as in her
ir	as in dirt
ur	as in burn

Explain to the child that when he sees these letter partners together, a new sound is made that is different from the individual letter sounds.

ACTIVITIES FOR GROUP 1 PARTNERS

1. COOKIE SHEETS FOR PARTNERS: It's time to get out the cookie sheet and magnetic letters again. This time, have the child make true CVC words, then let him remove the last letter and put an **r** in its place. Even if the words are nonsense, this is still great practice.

CVC . . . . PARTNERS

cat	. . . . car
fat	. . . . far
fog	. . . . for
sit	. . . . sir
bat	. . . . bar

Then, let the child make words in which a consonant follows the r. Demonstrate how to blend the letters together, remembering to use the partners as one sound.

ford	"f-or-d"	dart
turn		park
hurt		bird
cart		perk
dirt		term
burn		fort

Be sure to have the child read the words he makes.

2. HIGHLIGHT TIME: Make a list of more of these partner words mixed with some true CVC words. Have the child highlight in red marker those words that have partners. He can use yellow highlighter for the true CVC words. Then have him read the words to you. Here are some examples:

jerk	kid	fork	jar
red	jet	turf	pork
Kirk	sort	tug	rat
term	Tim	Bert	port

GROUP 2 PARTNERS: The next set of partners to be introduced will be those that combine two or more consonants (and sometimes a vowel, too). Educators seem to disagree on all of the letter combinations available, but this list of partners commonly found in our written language should serve the purpose well. Continue with an introductory phrase for each new partner. Choose a KEY

WORD for each set of letter partners. There are many suggestions listed in the following activities or you may use your own choice for a KEY WORD.

Example: Say, "These are the letter partners **cl.** Together, they cay **cl** as in **clip.**"

cl	gl	sk	squ	tr	nk	nt
br	gr	sl	st	tw	ph	pt
cr	pl	sm	str	ch	qu	mp
dr	pr	sn	sw	ck	sh	ct
fl	sc	sp	tch	ng	th	wh
spr	spl	scr	sch	dw	str	lb

ACTIVITIES FOR GROUP 2 PARTNERS

1. REPRISE SURPRISE!: Remember that you can use many of the activity ideas from the earlier chapters to practice these new partner sounds. Especially appropriate would be MAKE-A-WORD activities with the cookie sheet. For example, have the child make such words as:

blob	skid	duck
clip	slip	Nick
drip	snap	pack
drop	spit	chum
Fred	split	batch
glad	squid	sink
grin	stop	whip
plop	strip	quit
scat	twig	shot

Then add other partner combinations that use what the child learned in the GROUP 1 PARTNERS. For example:

smart	flirt
skirt	snort
shirt	spark
chirp	sharp
slurp	chart
third	sport

It would also be beneficial to make new game boards, Bingo cards, flashcards, configurations and story cards that use the new partners. Just update your games from the previous chapters. Continue to add words and patterns as the child progresses up the reading ladder.

2. PARTNER POKER: Use 3x5 file cards to make your own card game. Play a version of "Go Fish" with eight letter combinations. Write each combination on 4 file cards so that you have 32 cards, with 4 of each kind. After you have demonstrated each of the 8 sounds, shuffle the cards, deal 8 cards to each player and put the remaining cards in a pile face down. Continue to play as you would "Go Fish" with each person asking another for a specific sound. Note: You must make the SOUNDS of the letters and not just ask for the card by the names of the letters.

Once the child has mastered these sounds, add more

cards and play additional games until all the partners have been introduced. Obviously, this is an activity that requires several sessions just to introduce each of the partners. Later, isolate any of the partners which may be confusing the child and play the game using only those particular cards.

GROUP 3 PARTNERS: The next group of letter combinations to be introduced are those in which a vowel is followed by a consonant and then by a silent **e**. This pattern will be designated as VCE. Explain to the child that in this partnership, the silent **e** works its magic on the first vowel causing it to say its own name.

Example: Say, "The letter **a** with silent **e** at the end says **a** as in **cake**."

VCE PARTNERS

a   as in cake
e   as in Pete
i   as in ice
o   as in home
u   as in mule

ACTIVITIES FOR GROUP 3 PARTNERS

1. IT'S MAGIC AGAIN: Here's another opportunity for your child to perform his "magic." Let him

see what happens when he adds the letter **e** to the ends of those CVC words he now knows well.

Let him use marker board or cookie sheet to demonstrate his tricks as he changes the following words:

mat . . . . mate	bit . . . . . . bite
tap . . . . . tape	rip . . . . . . ripe
mop . . . . mope	sham . . . . . shame
tub . . . . . tube	cop . . . . . . cope
not . . . . . note	us . . . . . . use
kit . . . . . kite	gap . . . . . . gape
tam . . . . tame	cub . . . . . . cube
hat . . . . . hate	rob . . . . . . robe
dim . . . . dime	mad . . . . . made
pin . . . . . pine	cap . . . . . . cape
rat . . . . rate	pet . . . . . . Pete
hid . . . . hide	hop . . . . hope
slop . . . . slope	shin . . . . . shine
slid . . . . slide	cut . . . . . . cute

2. MORE STORY CARD FUN: The child will need opportunities to apply the new skills that he is learning. So, here are examples of practice stories that require the child to use the letters and sounds introduced in earlier chapters. Print these short stories on large file cards. Let the child illustrate each story. Note any difficulties that the child has so that you can re-teach with alternate activities. As always, be ready to create your own practice stories as well.

PETE AND THE KITE

Pete had a kite with red dots. It was a kit that cost ten dimes. Pete got on a hill and ran. The kite went up, but it hit a big pine! Then, it hit the dirt.

Pete did not mope. He got tape and a pin. He made the kite glide up past the pine. Pete had a lot of fun with the kite.

SLIM AND SLIME

Slim was a cute, white duck. Slim had a home on Lake Quack. On a hot day, Slim slid into the lake. Slim got stuck in wet black slime.

"Squish, squish!" went Slim in the slime.

Slim woke Fred the frog. Fred got a big thick rope to help Slim.

"Squish, squish!" Slim got on to the bank and he did not slide. Slim had a nap.

3. BOX IT!: Use the following activity to encourage mastery of these CVC and VCE letter partners and to teach your child to follow directions. Fold a piece of paper or a file card into 6 sections. Then, have the child listen to and follow these directions.

    1. In the top right-hand box, write the word **fame**.
    2. In the bottom left-hand box, write the word **trap**.
    3. In the top middle box, write the word **drop**.
    4. In the bottom right-hand box, write the word **shape**.
    5. In the top left-hand box, write the word **shrug**.
    6. In the bottom middle box, write the word **twine**.

shrug	drop	fame
trap	twine	shape

On another occasion, repeat this activity using nonsense words. These nonsense activities will demonstrate the child's level of understanding of skills taught thus far.

1. In the bottom left-hand box, write the word **flaz**.
2. In the top middle box, write the word **stibe**.
3. In the bottom right-hand box, write the word **plote**.

4. In the top left-hand box, write the word **zab**.
5. In the top right-hand box, write the word **slude**.
6. In the bottom middle box, write the word **tron**.

GROUP 4 PARTNERS: This next group of partners is made up of those in which 2 vowels work together or in which a prominent vowel and consonants work together to form a partnership. In this group there will be some partnerships that can make more than one possible sound. In those situations, the most common sound is listed first. This will not cause a problem for the child if the less common sounds are taught as options.

Example: Say, "The letter partners **ai** make the sound in **rain**."

ai   as in rain
ay   as in day
oa   as in boat
oe   as in toe
ee   as in feet
ea   as in eat, steak, or head
old as in cold
igh as in fight
ign as in sign
oo   as in moon or book
ou   as in ouch, soup, or couple
ow   as in cow or snow
au   as in Paul
aw   as in saw
ei   as in eight and either
oi   as in oil

oy   as in boy
ue   as in glue
ui   as in fruit
ew   as in few and sew
ey   as in key and they
ie   as in thief and died

ACTIVITIES FOR GROUP 4 PARTNERS

1. HOW CAN YOU MAKE IT?: Let the child figure out how many letter partners he can remember that make a certain sound. For example:

   1.) "Tell me 2 possible ways to make this sound: **oy** (as in boy)."

   Let him try to remember the letter partners; **oy** and **oi**. You may need to prompt him with some words that have that pattern to let him hear the sound in words.

   2.) "Think of at least 4 possible ways to make this sound: **a** (as in cake)."

   Hopefully, he will remember the letter partners: **ai, ay, a-e, ea,** and **ei.**

   3.) "Tell me 4 possible ways to make this sound: **o** (as in boat)."

He should come up with these partners:
oa, oe, ow, and **o-e.**

You can continue this activity with many different sounds and combinations.

2. BLANKITY-BLANK!: Use magnetic letters or let the child write on a chalkboard for this activity. From memory, he can choose from only the Group 4 Letter Partners to fill in these blanks. There can be more than one possible answer.

1.	j _ _	(joy, jaw)
2.	P _ _ l	(Paul)
3.	br _ _ l	(broil)
4.	pl _ _	(plow)
5.	j _ _ nt	(joint)
6.	gr _ _ ch	(grouch)
7.	cl _ _	(claw)
8.	cr _ _ l	(crawl)
9.	st _ _ t	(stout)
10.	br _ _ _ t	(bright)

Continue to create similar word blanks. Remember that the child will enjoy making a little activity like this for you, too!

3. LONG, LONGER, LONGEST!: Use a roll of paper such as a calculator or adding machine tape. With markers or crayons, have the child write some words that have the Group 4 Letter Partners. See how many of these he can write. Make this an on-

going project. It will be fun to write the letter partners in one color and to write the other letters in a second color. Show him how easy it is to do simple rhyming patterns by repeating the letter partners. For example: gain, main, pain, rain, vain, stain, strain, etc.

4. UPDATE: Use these words as you continue to update games from the earlier chapters.

train	fail	wait	sleep
soap	mail	slay	preach
new	nail	tray	goat
scold	pail	faint	throat
plain	sail	spray	boast
aid	tail	faith	croak
laid	bay	clay	grown
maid	day	saint	blow
raid	may	seem	feet
chain	stain	dream	bleed
brain	moist	scream	soil
strain	stay	squeal	howl
pouch	foil	point	ground
gown	crown	south	cloud
squeak	beach	shawl	draw
thaw	salt	law	hoe
launch	jaw	paint	toad
soak	blew	blue	threw
show	hold	bloom	fold
spook	smooth	root	chew
coin	fright	bold	high
right	cue	fowl	low

5. AUTHOR! AUTHOR!: Encourage your child to make his own stories using the CVC words, Letter Partners and Weird Words. He has a multitude of possibilities available to him. Let him share his creation with family members, other relatives or friends. Also, encourage him to record his story on a video or cassette. The more he uses words, the more he will understand how they work.

6. CEREAL CAPER: This game takes place on the cereal aisle at your local grocery store. In a very real setting, this activity will demonstrate the importance of ALL of the letter partners. Give the child a paper and pencil and ask him to locate the following letter partners on cereal boxes:

Partner	Possible Answers:
oa	oat, toasted
ea	wheat
ai	grain
cr	crunch, crisp
ow	low
qu	quick
ar	charm
oo	spoon
ew	new
a-e	flake
or	corn

You get the idea? You can make up your own list, of course, and expand it to any aisle of the grocery store. Or use your pantry, the toy store or sports store. Just helping the child to notice words and their patterns of letters will promote his motivation to learn even more.

MORE WEIRD WORDS

Remember those irregular words that just have to be memorized? Only 5 have been introduced so far, but here is a list of 20 more common ones. Introduce them in groups of 5 and do not move on to a new group until the child has mastered the previous one. Write them on file cards and do not forget the funny clouds that will set them apart.

1. where	1. you	1. work	1. from
2. have	2. could	2. were	2. laugh
3. one	3. because	3. two	3. your
4. does	4. again	4. above	4. who
5. they	5. some	5. there	5. want

Chapter 6

NOW, ABOUT THOSE LONG WORDS...!

As you probably have noticed, the emphasis up to this point has been on words with only one syllable. Once the child has a good understanding of the letters and sounds in these shorter and less complicated words, the multi-syllable words will usually pose little problem. He will be able to see that the longer words are really made up of smaller parts. He is able to use the skills he already knows to decode those more difficult words.

Helping the child to recognize syllables can be fun! Here are some activities that will help the child to first HEAR the syllables and then to SEE the parts within longer words. With practice, he will soon become skillful at visual/auditory recognition. Once the child has a thorough understanding of the very basic stages, these next steps become almost automatic.

GAMES AND ACTIVITIES FOR CHAPTER 6

1. EXAGGERATE AND CLAP IT: In order to help the child hear separate syllables, pronounce the

word in very distinctive parts. For example:

entertain . . . . Say "en   ter   tain."

Exaggerate each part so that the child can hear the individual syllables. Then have the child clap once for each syllable as he says it. Practice this routine on all kinds of words: family names, cities and states, names of schools, etc. Continue to do this activity orally so that the child will be able to clap any word independently. It is fun to try this activity when you are driving down the street. Use the words on street signs or billboard signs.

2. SYLLABLE SILLIES!: Using the following list of nonsense words, have the child pronounce each word and count the number of syllables. Have him clap each syllable if he has any trouble. Then, let him use a marker to circle each syllable within the word. If he needs assistance, cover the second syllable with your finger while he reads the first. Then uncover the second syllable (or third) and have him read it.

As another entertaining way to use nonsense words for teaching syllables, let the child create his own nonsense words for household items or food items. He will enjoy eating **goozbock** instead of peanut butter! In fact, he could make up an entire menu of nonsense words to be posted for the evening meal.

zibdee
trabshaw
meaderzee
flibadzoo
troig
traimlawpoo
stridderpaft
loogtudder
stight
flavraim

3. PRACTICE MAKES PERFECT!: The best way to use the skills from earlier chapters is to read, read, READ! Use simple story books from the library. You may want to share the reading with the child. If he has difficulty with a word, TRY NOT TO FILL IN THE APPROPRIATE RESPONSE FOR HIM! Silently hold your finger under the word or cover the other syllables while he sounds out the syllables one by one. Show him how to take apart the word. From time to time you may need to prompt him with a question such as, "What sound does that make?" or "Do you see letter partners here? What do they say?"

When the word that stumps him is irregular, simply tell him the word and let him continue. If he is frustrated by the difficulty of too many words, it may be that he has not quite mastered the basic levels. Do not be disheartened. Return to the activities in the earlier chapters for reinforcement. As he matures as a reader, you will sense when he is able to move ahead. REMEMBER, keep the atmosphere pleasant and fun for the best results.

END IT WITH....:

One more way to help the child with more complex words is to familiarize him with common word endings that will appear often in written words. It may be helpful to first circle these endings in words or to just point them out as the child reads. Very quickly, he will come to recognize them as special endings.

-ture	as in picture
-tion	as in action
-tious	as in cautious
-sure	as in treasure
-sion	as in mansion
-cial	as in special
-ive	as in detective
-ing	as in fishing
-y	as in crazy
-le	as in apple
-ed	as in needed or jumped
-ly	as in gladly
-ous	as in dangerous
-ance	as in importance

POWER BOOSTER ACTIVITIES

The following list includes activities that will directly or indirectly promote your child's reading progress. These activities are easy-to-do, require little planning and provide meaningful learning experiences. You can do them with your child while driving, shopping or even waiting in a restaurant. These ideas might boost you into creating your own activities as well.

Ask your child to:

1. ...write some of his newly-mastered letters or words on paper napkins to be used for the family dinner. He will be thrilled to show off his work!

2. ...locate and circle certain letters or words on the disposable children's menus often found in restaurants. Example: "How many **g's** can you find on this page?" "Can you find **hot dog** on this menu?"

3. ...find certain letters or words on street signs, highway signs, or billboards. Example: "Can you find the word **exit**?"

4. ...notice words written on the instrument panel of your car. You can use these words to locate individual letters or to find letter partners (**heat, vent, temperature,** etc.).

5. ...write the words for the items on your grocery or things-to-do list. Let him use his newly-learned skills to sound out such words as **milk**, **eggs**, **bread**, etc. Remind him of letter partners if he need help. If a word simply does not adhere to its true sounds, just explain that it is another example of a WEIRD WORD.

6. ...fill in the family calendar with names and events. The more he writes, the more familiar he will be with the reading/writing relationship.

7. ...complete a sequencing pattern made from coins. Use pennies, nickels, dimes and quarters to make your own pattern, then have the child complete the pattern. Ask him, "What comes next?" Provide him with coins to continue the pattern.

8. ...solve grocery store riddles.

    I am white.
    I am sweet.
    You can find me in a bag.
    What am I?   (sugar or sugar-substitute)

    I am very cold.
    I come in different flavors.
    Most children really like me.
    What am I?   (ice cream)

Create your own riddles for your shopping list. Increase the difficulty as the child is able. This activity will build both vocabulary and thinking skills.

9. ...identify which direction you are turning when driving the car. As you push the blinkers and prepare to turn the car, ask your child, "Which way are we turning?"

Chapter 7

HE IS WELL ON HIS WAY!

When all the skills presented in this book are introduced, reinforced and mastered, the child should have a tremendous understanding of how words work. He should be comfortable with reading all regular words and a number of irregular words taught as Weird Words. Even words that vary slightly from their true sounds will probably cause little problem for him.

Often children lose interest in reading because the materials in their basal readers are too contrived and uninteresting. In school, much of the reading class time may be spent completing workbook pages and written exercises while little time is actually spent reading! However, if your child has mastered the basic skills in this book, he should no longer be tied to repetitive practice of disjointed skills. He should be ready for the world of literature, billboards, signs, song lyrics, magazines, comics, menus, cookbook instructions and on and on!

The child should also be ready for more specific tasks that involve sequencing, summarizing, deductive thinking, vocabulary expansion, context clues, finding the main idea and probable outcomes. These skills require a child's ability to recognize and pronounce unfamiliar words so that he is able to determine the message of the words. He will also be prepared to begin more technical word structures. With this foundation as a beginning reader, he is ready to expand his world of written words.

As he grows as a reader, he will be able to read independently and silently. However, you can continue to be very involved with the child's progress. There are ways that you can check the child's level of comprehension as well as spark his higher level thinking skills. After he has read a story or passage, ask him to predict what might happen next in the story. You might also have him retell a story that he has read.

In conclusion, this book was designed to give a beginning reader a meaningful and practical foundation. In a logical order, the sounds of the letters and letter partners have been introduced and reinforced. This process is very systematic and controlled in its early stages; however, that foundation now provides the child the freedom to read just about anything he would like. Once the child has mastered the basic steps, he should be able to read from an endless supply of materials. He should also be able to spell and write with confidence. You have given him a most precious gift! Congratulations!

ABOUT THE AUTHOR

Melisa Buchanan is an experienced primary teacher and academic therapist with a graduate degree from the University of North Texas. She has been involved as an educational consultant and tutor in the Dallas - Ft. Worth area where she lives with her husband and three children. She also continues to work as a reading resource volunteer in a local public school district.

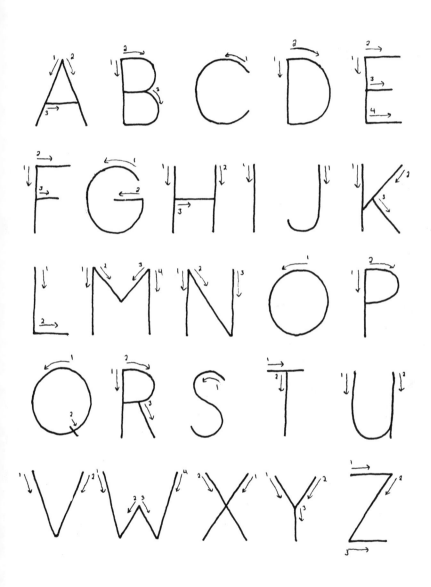

NOTES

NOTES

NOTES

NOTES

NOTES

NOTES

NOTES

NOTES

NOTES

NOTES

NOTES